ISBN: 978129004556

Published by:
HardPress Publishing
8345 NW 66TH ST #2561
MIAMI FL 33166-2626

Email: info@hardpress.net
Web: http://www.hardpress.net

WAR BRIDES

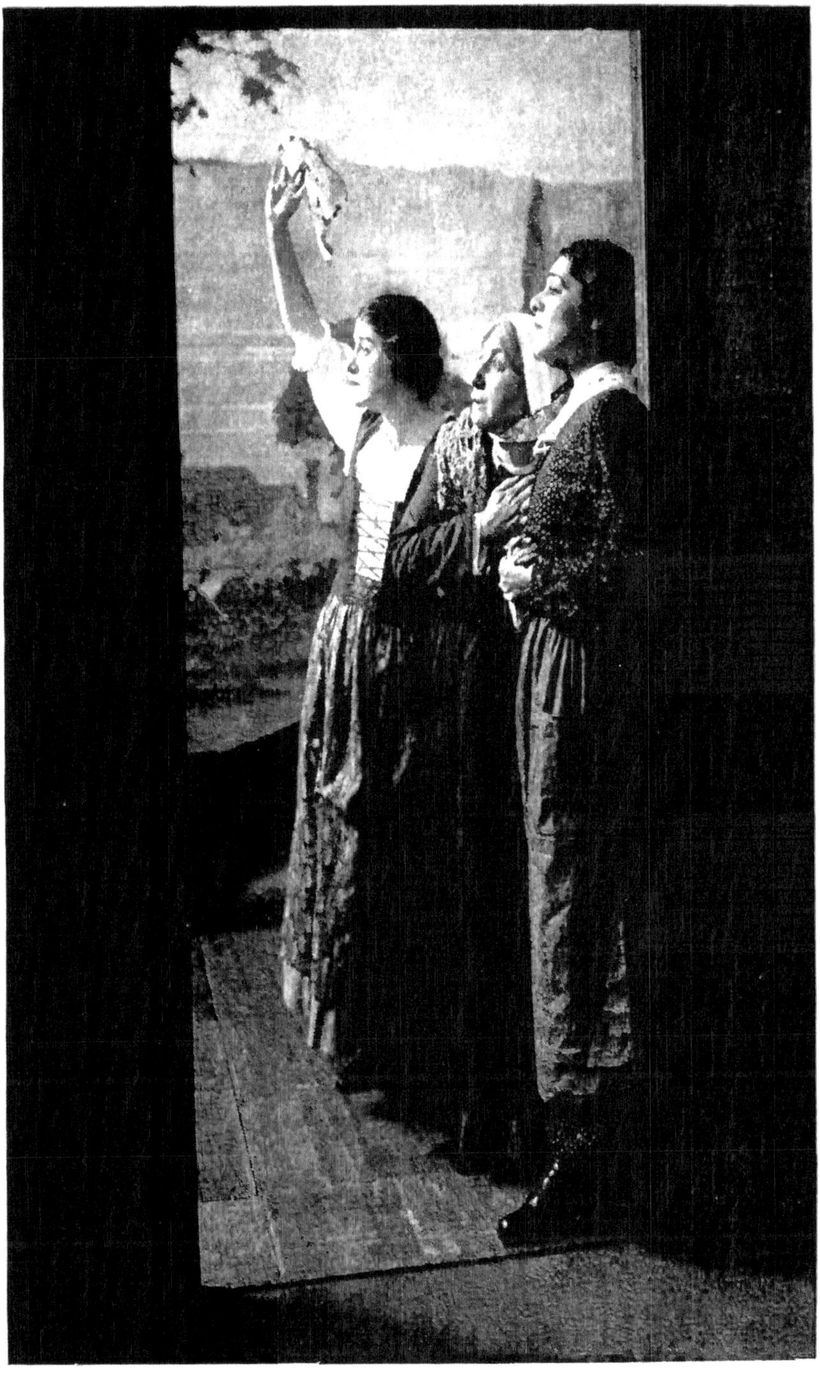

Good-by! good-by!

WAR BRIDES

A Play in One Act

BY

MARION GRAIG WENTWORTH

ILLUSTRATED WITH PHOTOGRAPHS FROM THE
PLAY AS PRESENTED BY MME. NAZIMOVA

NEW YORK
THE CENTURY CO.
1915

Published, February 1915

TO

MY LITTLE BOY

BRANDON

LIST OF ILLUSTRATIONS

This play was first produced
on January 25, 1915, at

B. F. KEITH'S PALACE THEATRE,
NEW YORK CITY,

with the following cast:

Hedwig (Joan)..................Mme. Nazimova
Amelia (Amy).....................Mary Alden
Mother ....Gertrude Berkeley
Hoffman (Joseph Kerman)........Charles Bryant
Minna ....Edith Speare
Arno ....C. Brown
Hertz (Captain Bragg)..........William Hasson
Peasants, Women and Soldiers.

Time—Present.   Place—A War-Ridden Country.

Personal Manager for Madame Nazimova
William F. Muenster

WAR BRIDES

WAR BRIDES

The war brides were cheered with enthusiasm and the churches were crowded when the wedding parties spoke the ceremony in concert.—PRESS CLIPPING.

SCENE: *A room in a peasant's cottage in a war-ridden country. A large fireplace at the right. Near it a high-backed settle. On the left a heavy oak table and benches. Woven mats on the floor. A door at left leads into a bedroom. In the corner a cupboard. At the back a wide window with scarlet geraniums and an open door. A few firearms are stacked near the fireplace. There is an air of homely color and neatness about the room.*

Through the open door may be seen women

3

stacking grain. Others go by carrying huge baskets of grapes or loads of wood, and gradually it penetrates the mind that all these workers are women, aristocrats and peasants side by side. Now and then a bugle blows or a drum beats in the distance. A squad of soldiers marches quickly by. There is everywhere the tense atmosphere of unusual circumstance, the anxiety and excitement of war.

Amelia, a slight, flaxen-haired girl of nineteen, comes in. She brushes off the hay with which she is covered, and goes to packing a bag with a secret, but determined, air. The Mother passes the window and appears in the doorway. She is old and work-worn, but sturdy and stoical. Now she carries a heavy load of wood, and is weary. She casts a sharp eye at Amelia.

Mother:

What are you doing, girl? [*Amelia starts and puts the bag in the cupboard.*] Who's going away? They have n't sent for Arno?

Amelia:

No.

Mother:

[*Sighs, and drops her load on the hearth.*] Is the hay all in?

Amelia:

Yes. I put in the last load. All the big work on our place is done, and so—[*Looks at her mother and hesitates. Her mother begins to chop the wood into kindling.*] I 'll do that, Mother.

Mother:

Let be, girl. It keeps me from worrying. Get a bite to eat. What were you doing with that bag? Who were you packing it for?

Amelia:

[*With downcast eyes.*]

Myself.

Mother: [*Anxious.*]

What for?

Amelia:

Sit down, Mother, and be still while I tell you—

[*Pushes her mother into a chair.*]

Mother: [*Starts.*]

Is there any news? Quick! Tell me!

Amelia:

Not since yesterday. Only they say Franz is at the front. We don't know where Emil and Otto are, and there's been a battle; but—

Mother:

[*Murmurs, with closed eyes.*]

My boys! my boys!

Amelia:

Don't, Mother! They may come back.
[*A cheer is heard.*]

Mother: [*Starting.*]

What's that?

Amelia:

[*Running to the door and looking out.*]
They are cheering the war brides, that's all.

Mother:

Aye. There's been another wedding ceremony.

Amelia:

Yes.

Mother:

How many war brides to-day?

Amelia:

Ten, they said.

Mother: [*Nodding.*]

Aye, that is good. Has any one asked you, Amelia? [*Amelia looks embarrassed.*] Some one should ask you. You are a good-looking girl.

Amelia: [*In a low voice.*]

Hans Hoffman asked me last night.

Mother:

The young and handsome lieutenant? You are lucky. You said yes?

Amelia: [*Shakes her head.*]

No.

Mother:

Ah, well.

Amelia:

I hardly know him. I've only spoken to him once before. O Mother—that is n't what I want to do.

Mother:

What did you tell him?

Amelia: [*Timidly.*]

That I was going away to join the Red Cross.

Mother:

Amelia!

Amelia:

He did n't believe me. He kissed me—and I ran away.

Mother:

The Red Cross!

Amelia: [*Eagerly.*]

Yes; that is what I was going to tell you just now. That is why I was packing the bag. [*Gets it.*] I—I want to go. I want to go to-night. I can't stand this waiting.

Mother:

You leave me, too?

Amelia:

I want to go to the front with Franz and Otto and Emil, to nurse them, to take care of them if they are wounded—and all the others. Let me, Mother! I, too, must do something for my country. The grapes are plucked, and the hay is stacked. Hedwig is gathering the wheat. You can spare me. I have been dreaming of it night and day.

Mother:
[*Setting her lips decisively.*]

No, Amelia!

Amelia:

O Mother, why?

Mother:

You must help me with Hedwig. I can't manage her alone.

Amelia:

Hedwig!

Mother:

She is strange; she broods. Had n't you no-
ticed?

Amelia:

Why, yes; but I thought she was worrying
about Franz. She adores him, and any day she
may hear that he is killed. It 's the waiting
that 's so awful.

Mother:

But it 's more than the waiting with Hedwig.
Aye, you will help Franz more by staying home
to take care of his wife, Amelia, especially now.

Amelia: [*Puzzled.*]
Now?

Mother:
          [*Goes to her work-basket.*]
Hedwig has told you nothing?

Amelia:

No.

Mother:

Ah, she is a strange girl! She asked me to keep it a secret,—I don't know why,—but now I think you should know. See!

[*Very proudly she holds up the tiny baby garments she is knitting.*]

Amelia:
[*Pleased and astonished.*]

So Franz and Hedwig—

Mother: [*Nods.*]

For their child. In six months now. My first grandchild, Amelia. Franz's boy, perhaps. I shall hear a little one's voice in this house again.

Amelia:
[*Uncertainly, as she looks at the little things.*]

Still—I want to go.

Mother: [*Firmly.*]

We must take care of Hedwig, Amelia. She is to be a mother. That is our first duty. It is our only hope of an heir if you won't marry soon—and if—if the boys don't come back.

Amelia:

Arno is left.

Mother:

Ah, but they'll be calling him next. It is his birthday to-day, too, poor lad. He's on the jump to be off. I see him gone, too. God knows I may never see one of them again. I sit here in the long evenings and think how death may take my boys,—even this minute they may be breathing their last,—and then I knit this baby sock and think of the precious little life that's coming. It's my one comfort, Amelia. Nothing must happen now.

Amelia:

[*With a touch of impatience.*]
What's the matter with Hedwig?

Mother:

I don't know what it is. She acts as if she did n't want to bring her child into the world. She talks wild. I tell you I must have that child, Amelia! I cannot live else. Hedwig frightens me. The other night I found her sitting on the edge of her bed staring,—when she should have been asleep,—as if she saw visions, and whispering, "I will send a message to the emperor." What message? I had to shake her out of it. She refuses to make a thing for her baby. Says, "Wait till I see what they do to Franz." It's unnatural.

Amelia:

I can't understand her. I never could. I always thought it was because she was a factory-town girl.

Mother:

If anything should happen to Franz in the state she's in now, Hedwig might go out of her mind entirely. So you had best stay by, Amelia. We must keep a close eye on her.

[*There is a knock at the door.*]

Who's that?

Amelia:

[*Looks out of the windows, and then whispers.*]

It's Hans Hoffman.

[*The knock is repeated.*]

Mother:

Open, girl! Don't stand there!

[*Enter Hoffman, gay, familiar, inclined to*

stoutness, but good-looking. Accustomed to having the women bow down to him.]

Hoffman:

[*To Amelia.*] Ah, ha! You gave me the slip yesterday!

Amelia:

My mother.

Hoffman: [*Nodding.*]

Good day, Mother. [*She curtsies.*]

[*Coming closer to Amelia.*]

Where did you run to? Here she as good as promised me she would wed me to-day, Mother, and then—

Amelia:

Oh, no!

Hoffman:

Yes, you did. You let me kiss you.

Amelia: [*Taken aback.*]

Oh, sir!

Hoffman:

And when I got to the church square to-day, no bride for Hans Hoffman. Well, I must say, they had the laugh on me; for I had told them I had found the girl for me—the prettiest bride of the lot. But to-morrow——

Amelia:

I can't.

Hoffman:

[*Taking hold of her.*]

Oh, yes, you can. I won't bother you long. I'm off to the front any day now. Come, promise me! What do you say, Mother?

Mother: [*Slowly.*]

I should like to see her wed.

Hoffman:

There!

Amelia:

[*Shrinking from both him and the idea.*]
But I don't know you well enough yet.

Hoffman:

Well, look me over. Don't you think I am good enough for her, Mother? Besides, we can't stop to think of such things now, Amelia. It is war-time. This is an emergency measure. And, then, I'm a soldier—like to die for my country. That ought to count for something—a good deal, I should say—if you love your country, and you do, don't you, Amelia?

Amelia:

Oh, yes!

Hoffman:

Well, then, we can get married and get acquainted afterward.

Amelia: *[Faintly.]*

I wanted to be a nurse.

Hoffman:

Nonsense! Pretty girls like you should marry. The priests and the generals have commanded it. It's for the fatherland. Ought she not to wed me, Mother?

Mother:

[Nodding impersonally.]

Aye, it is for the fatherland they ask it.

Hoffman:

Of course. It is your patriotic duty, Amelia. You're funny. All the young women are tickled at the chance. But you are the one I have picked out, and I am going to have you. Now, there's a good girl—promise!

[*A hubbub of voices and a cheer are heard out-*

side. Enter Minna, flushed, pretty, light headed.]

Amelia:

Minna!

Minna:
[Holding out her hand.]

Amelia, see! My wedding-ring!

Amelia:

Iron!

Minna: *[Triumphantly.]*

Yes; a war bride!

Amelia:

You?

Minna:

That's what I am. *[Whirling gaily about.]*

Hoffman:
[Shaking her hand.]

Good for you! Congratulations!

Minna:

Did n't you hear them cheer? That was for me!

Hoffman:

There 's patriotism for you, Amelia!

Amelia:

When were you married, Minna?

Minna:

Just now. There were ten of us. We all answered in chorus. It was fun—just like a theater. Then the priest made a speech, and the burgomaster and the captain. The people cheered, and then our husbands had to go to drill for an hour. Oh, I never was so thrilled! It was grand! They told us we were the true patriots.

Hoffman:

Hurrah! And so you are.

Minna:

Our names will go down in history, honored by a whole people, they said.

[*They are all carried away by Minna's enthusiasm; even Amelia warms up.*]

Amelia:

But whom did you marry, Minna?

Minna:

Heinrich Berg.

Amelia:　　　　　[*Dubious.*]

That loafer!

Minna:

He's all right. He's a soldier now. Why, he may be a hero, fighting for the fatherland; and that makes a lot of difference, Amelia.

Hoffman:

What did I tell you?

Minna:

I probably would n't have picked him out in peace-times, but it is different now. He only asked me last night. Of course he may get killed. They said we 'd have a widow's pension fund,—us and our children,—forever and ever, if the boys did n't come back. So, you see, I won't be out anything. Anyway, it 's for the country. We 'll be famous, as war brides. Even the name sounds glorious, does n't it? War bride! Is n't that fine?

Hoffman:

Here 's a little lady who will hear herself called that to-morrow. [*Takes Amelia's hand.*]

Minna:

[*Clapping her hands.*]

Amelia a war bride, too! Good!

Hoffman:

You 'll be proud to hear her called that, won't you, Mother?   Give us your blessing.

Minna:

I 'd rather be a wife or a widow any day than be an old maid; and to be a war bride—oh!

[*Amelia is blushing and tremulous.*]

Mother:

[*With a far-away look.*]

It is for the fatherland, Amelia.   Aye, aye, the masters have said so.   It is the will and judgment of those higher than us.   They are wise. Our country will need children. Aye. Say yes, my daughter.   You will not say no when your country bids you!   It is your emperor, your country, who asks, more than Hans Hoffman.

Amelia:

[*Impressed, and questions herself to see if her patriotism is
strong enough to stand the test,
while Hoffman, charmed by
Amelia's gentleness, is moved by
more personal feeling.*]

Hoffman:

[*Kissing Amelia on both cheeks.*]
There, it's all settled. [*A faint cheer is heard
without.*] To-morrow they will cheer you like
that; and when I go, I shall have a bride to
wave me good-by instead of—

[*Enter Hedwig.*

*She stands in the doorway, looking out on the
distant crowds. She is tall, well built, and
carries herself proudly. Strong, intelligent
features, but pale. Her eyes are large with*

*anxiety.   She has soft, wavy black hair.   An
inward flame seems to be consuming her.
The sounds continue in the distance, cheering,
disputing mingled with far bugle-calls and
marching feet.*]

Hedwig:

[*Contemptuously.*]

Ha!

[*The sound startles the others.   They turn.*]

All:

Hedwig!

Hedwig:

[*Still in the doorway, looking out.*]

War brides!

Minna: [*Pertly.*]

You 're a war bride yourself, Hedwig.

Hedwig:

[*Turns quickly, locates Minna, almost springs at her.*]

Don't you dare to call me a war bride! My ring is gold. See. [*Seizes Minna's hand, and then throws it from her.*] Not iron, like yours.

Minna:

[*Boldly taunting.*]

They even call you the first war bride.

Hedwig:

[*Furious, towering over her, her hand on her shoulder.*]

Say why, why?

Minna: [*Weakening.*]

Because you were the first one to be married when the war broke out.

Hedwig:

[*Both hands on her shoulders.*]

Because the Government commanded? Because they bribed me with the promise of a widow's pension? Tell the truth.

*Minna:*ˊ   [*Faintly.*]

No.   Let me go.

Hedwig:

So! And how long had Franz and I been engaged? Now say.

Minna:

[*Beginning to be frightened.*]

Two years.

Hedwig:

[*Flinging her off.*]

Of course. Everybody knows it. Every village this side the river knew we were to be married this summer. We 've dreamed and worked for nothing else all these months. It had nothing to do with the war—our love, our marriage. So, you see, I am no war bride. [*Walks scornfully away.*] Not like you, anyway.

[*They all stare at her.*]

Hoffman:

[*Stepping forward indignantly.*] I don't know why you should have this contempt for our war brides, and speak like that.

Hedwig:

[*Sits down, half turned away. She shrugs her shoulders, and her lips curl in a little smile.*]

Hoffman:

They are coming to the rescue of their country. Saving it; else it will perish.

Hedwig: [*Bitterly.*]

Ha!

Hoffman:

[*Waxing warmer.*]

They are the saviors of the future.

Hedwig:　　　[*Sadly.*]

The future!

Mother:

[*Softly, laying her hand on Hedwig's shoulder.*]

Hedwig, be more respectful. Herr Hoffman is a lieutenant.

Hoffman:

When we are gone,—the best of us,—what will the country do if it has no children?

Hedwig:

Why did n't you think of that before—before you started this wicked war?

Hoffman:

I tell you it is a glory to be a war bride. There!

Hedwig: [*With a shrug.*]
A breeding-machine! [*They all draw back.*]
Why not call it what it is? Speak the naked
truth for once.

Hoffman:
You'll take that back to-morrow, when your sister stands up in the church with me.

Hedwig: [*Starting up.*]
Amelia? Marry you? No! Amelia, is this
true?

Amelia:
[*Hesitating, troubled, and uncertain.*]
They tell me I must—for the fatherland.

Hedwig:
Marry this man, whom you scarcely know,
whom surely you cannot love! Why, you make
a mock of marriage! It is n't that they have
tempted you with the widow's pension? It is

so tiny; it's next to nothing. Surely you
would n't yield to that?

Amelia: [*Frightened.*]
I did want to go as a nurse, but the priests and
the generals—they say we must marry—to—
for the fatherland, Hedwig.

Hoffman: [*To Hedwig.*]
I command you to be silent!

Hedwig:
Not when my sister's happiness is at stake.   If
you come back, she will have to live with you
the rest of her life.

Hoffman:
That is n't the question now.   We are going
away—the best of us—to be shot, most likely.
Don't you suppose we want to send some part
of ourselves into the future, since we can't live

ourselves? There, that's straight; and right, too.

Hedwig:

[*Nodding slowly.*]
What I said—to breed a soldier for the empire; to restock the land. [*Fiercely.*] And for what? For food for the next generation's cannon. Oh, it is an insult to our womanhood! You violate all that makes marriage sacred! [*Agitated, she walks about the room.*] Are we women never to get up out of the dust? You never asked us if we wanted this war, yet you ask us to gather in the crops, cut the wood, keep the world going, drudge and slave, and wait, and agonize, lose our all, and go on bearing more men—and more—to be shot down! If we breed the men for you, why don't you let us say what is to become of them? Do we want them shot—the very breath of our life?

Hoffman:

It is for the fatherland.

Hedwig:

You use us, and use us—dolls, beasts of bur-
den, and you expect us to bear it forever
dumbly; but I won't!   I shall cry out till I die.
And now you say it almost out loud, "Go and
breed for the empire."   War brides!   Pah!
[*Minna gasps, beginning to be terrified.   Hoffman rages.   Mother gazes with anxious con-
cern.   Amelia turns pale.*]

Hoffman:

I never would dream of speaking of Amelia like
that.   She is the sweetest girl I have seen for
many a day.

Hedwig:

What will happen to Amelia?   Have you
thought of that?   No; I warrant you have n't.

Well, look. A few kisses and sweet words, the
excitement of the ceremony, the cheers of the
crowd, some days of living together,—I won't
call it marriage, for Franz and I are the ones
who know what real marriage is, and how sacred
it is,—then what? Before you know it, an
order to march. Amelia left to wait for her
child. No husband to wait with her, to watch
over her. Think of her anxiety, if she learns
to love you! What kind of child will it be?
Look at me. What kind of child would *I*
have, do you think? I can hardly breathe for
thinking of my Franz, waiting, never knowing
from minute to minute. From the way I feel,
I should think my child would be born mad,
I'm that wild with worrying. And then for
Amelia to go through the agony alone! No
husband to help her through the terrible hour.
What solace can the state give then? And

after that, if you don't come back, who is going to earn the bread for her child?   Struggle and struggle to feed herself and her child; and the fine-sounding name you trick us with—war bride! Humph! that will all be forgotten then.   Only one thing can make it worth while, and do you know what that is?   Love.   We'll struggle through fire and water for that; but without it—   [*Gesture.*]

Hoffman:

[*Drawing Amelia to him.*]
Don't listen to her, Amelia.

Amelia:

[*Pushing Hoffman violently from her, runs from the room.*]
No, no, I can't marry you! I won't! I won't!

[*She shuts the door in his face.*]

Hedwig:

[*Triumphantly.*]

She will never be your war bride, Hans Hoffman!

Hoffman:

[*Suddenly, angrily.*]

By thunder! I 've made a discovery. You 're the woman! You 're the woman!

Hedwig:

What woman?

Hoffman:

Yesterday there were twenty war brides. The day before there were nearly thirty. To-day there were only ten. There are rumors— [*Excitedly.*] I 'll report you. They 'll find you guilty. I myself can prove it.

Hedwig:

Well?

Hoffman:

I heard them say at the barracks that some one
was talking the women out of marrying. They
did n't know who; but they said if they caught
her—caught any one talking as you have just
now, daring to question the wisdom of the emperor and his generals, the church, too,—she 'd
be guilty of treason. You are working against
the emperor, against the fatherland. Here you
have done it right before my very eyes; you
have taken Amelia right out of my arms.
You 're the woman who 's been upsetting the
others, and don't you deny it.

Hedwig:

Deny it? I am proud of it.

Hoffman:

Then the place for you is in jail. Do you
know what will be the end of you?

Hedwig:

[*Suddenly far away.*]

Yes, I know, if Franz does not come back. I know; but first [*Clenching her hands*] I must get my message to the empèror.

Hoffman: [*Very angry.*]

You will be shot for treason.

Hedwig:

[*Coming back, laughing slightly.*]

Shot? Oh, no, Herr Hans, you 'd never shoot me!

Hoffman:

Why not?

Hedwig:

Do I have to tell you, stupid? I am a woman: I can get in the crops; I can keep the country going while you are away fighting, and, most important, I might give you a soldier for your next army—for the kingdom. Don't you see my value? [*Laughs strangely.*] Oh, no, you'd never shoot me!

Mother:

There, there, don't excite her, sir.

Hedwig:

[*Her head in her hands, on the table.*] God! I wish you would shoot me! If you don't give me back my Franz! I've no mind to bring a son into the world for this bloody thing you call war.

Hoffman:

I am going straight to headquarters to report you.

[*Starts to go.*

Enter Arno excitedly. He is boyish and fair, in his early twenties, and looks even younger than he really is.]

Arno: [*To Hoffman.*]

There's an order to march at once—your regiment.

Hoffman:

Now?

Arno:

At once. You are wanted. They told me to tell you.

[*Hoffman moves with military precision to the door; then turns to Hedwig.*]

Hoffman:

I shall take the time to report you.
[*Goes.*]

Minna: [*To Arno.*]

Does Heinrich's regiment go, too?

Arno:

Heinrich who?

Minna:

Heinrich Berg.

Arno:

No. To-morrow.

[*Minna, now thoroughly scared, is slinking to
the door when Hedwig stops her.*]

Hedwig:

Ha! little Minna, why do you run so fast?
Heinrich does not go until to-morrow. [*Looks
at her thoughtfully.*]   Are you going to be able
to fight it through, little Minna, when the hard
days come? If you do give the empire a soldier, will it be any comfort to know you are
helping the falling birth-rate?

Minna: [*Shivering.*]

Oh, I am afraid of you!

Hedwig:

Afraid of the truth, you mean. You see it
at last in all its brutal bareness. Poor little
Minna! [*She puts her arm around Minna*

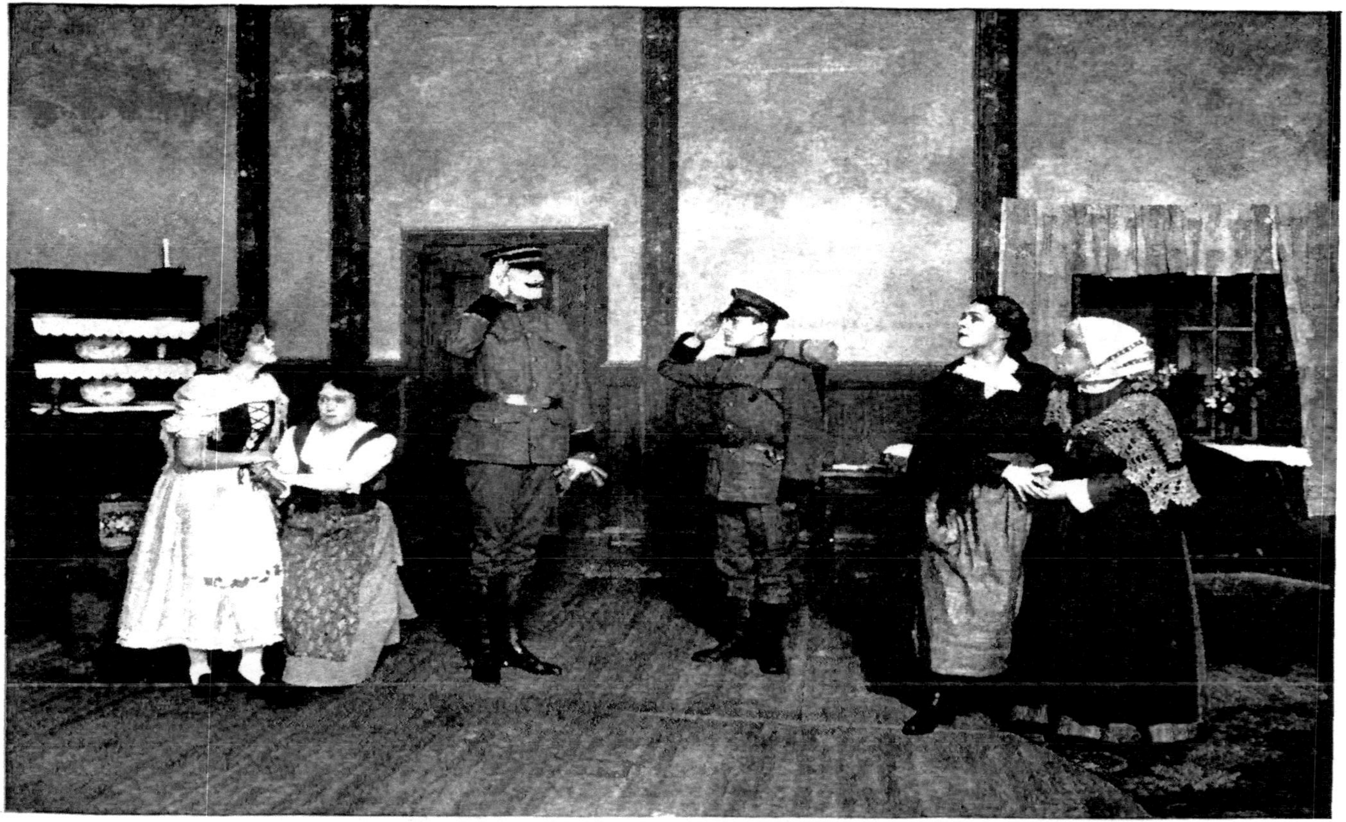

ARNO: You are wanted.

with sudden tenderness.] But you need not be afraid of me, little Minna. Oh, no. The trouble with me is I want no more war. Franz is at the war. I'm half mad with dreaming they have killed him. Any moment I may hear. If you loved your man as I do mine, little Minna, you'd understand. Well, go now, and to-morrow say good-by to your hus-band—of a day.

[*Minna, with a frightened backward glance, runs out the door.*

Arno, who has been talking in low tones to his mother, now rises.]

Arno:

Well, Mother, I have n't much time.

[*She clings to his hand.*]

Hedwig: [*Starting.*]

Arno!

Arno:

I am going, too.   Get those little things for me, Mother, will you?

Mother:

[*Goes to door and calls.*]

Amelia!   Come.   Arno has been called.

[*Amelia comes in.   Each in turn embraces him, sadly, but bravely.   Then the mother and sister gather together handkerchiefs, linen, writing-pad and pencil, and small necessaries.*]

Arno:

I have only a few minutes.

Hedwig: [*Tenderly.*]

Arno, my little brother, oh, why—why must you go?   You seem so young.

Arno:

I'm a man, like the others; don't forget

that, Hedwig. Be brave—to help me to be brave.

. [*They sit on the settle.*]

Hedwig:

[*Sighing.*]

Yes, it cannot be helped. Will you see my Franz, Arno? You look so like him to-day— the day I first saw him in the fields, the day of the factory picnic. It seems long ago. Tell him how happy he made me, and how I loved him. He did n't believe in this war no more than I, yet he had to go. He dreaded lest he meet his friends on the other side. You re- member those two young men from across the border? They worked all one winter side by side in the factory with Franz. They went home to join their regiments when the war was let loose on us. He never could stand it, Franz could n't, if he were ordered to drive

his·bayonet into them.   [*Gets up, full of emotion that is past expression.*]   Oh, it is too
monstrous!   And for what—for what?

Arno:

It is our duty.   We belong to the fatherland.
I would willingly give my life for my country.

Hedwig:

I would willingly give mine for peace.

Arno:

I must go.   Good-by, Hedwig.

Hedwig:

[*Controlling her emotion as she kisses him.*]
Good-by, my brave, splendid little brother.

Amelia:

I may come to the front, too.
[*They embrace tenderly.*]

Mother:

[*Strong and quiet, unable to speak, holds his head against her breast for a moment.*]

Fight well, my son.

Arno:

Yes, Mother.

[*He tears himself away. The silent suffering of the mother is pitiful. Her hands are crossed on her breast, her lips are seen to move in prayer. It is Hedwig who takes her in her arms and comforts her.*]

Hedwig:

And this is war—to tear our hearts out like this! Make mother some tea, Amelia, can't you?

[*Amelia prepares the cup of tea for her mother.*]

Mother:

[*After a few moments composes herself.*]
There, I am right now. I must remember—
and you must help me, my daughters—it is for
the fatherland.

Hedwig:

[*On her knees by the fire, shakes
her head slowly.*]
I wonder, I wonder. O Mother, I 'm not pa-
tient like you. I could n't stand it. To have
a darling little baby and see him grow into a
man, and then lose him like this! I 'd rather
never see the face of my child.

Mother:

We have them for a little while. I am thankful to God for what I have had.

Hedwig:

Then I must be very wicked.

Mother:

Are you sleeping better now, child?

Hedwig:

No; I am thinking of Franz.   He may be lying there alone on the battle-field, with none to help, and I here longing to put my arms around him.

[*Buries her face on the mother's knees and sobs.*]

Mother:

Hush, Hedwig!   Be brave!   Take care of yourself!   We must see that Franz's child is well born.

Hedwig:

If Franz returns, yes; if not—I—

[*Gets up impulsively, as if to run out of the house.*]

Amelia:

Don't you want your tea, Hedwig?

[*Hedwig throws open the door, and suddenly confronts a man who apparently was about to enter the house. He is an official, the military head of the town, known as Captain Hertz. He is well along in years, rheumatic, but · tremendously self-important.*]

Hertz:

[*Stopping Hedwig.*]

Wait one moment.   You are the young woman I wish to see.   You don't get away from me like that.

Hedwig:

[*Drawing herself up, moves back a step or two.*]

What is it?

Hertz:

[*Turning to the old mother.*]
Well, Maria, another son must go—Arno.
You are an honored woman, a noble example to
the state. [*Turns to Amelia.*] You have lost
a very good husband, I understand. Well,
you are a foolish girl. As for you [*Turning
to Hedwig, and eyeing her critically and se-
verely*], I hear pretty bad things. Yes, you
have been talking to the women—telling them
not to marry, not to multiply. In so doing
you are working directly against the Government. It is the express request and command
that our soldiers about to be called to the front
and our young women should marry. You de-
liberately set yourself in opposition to that command. Are you aware that that is treason?

Hedwig:
Why are they asking this, Herr Captain?

Hertz:

Our statesmen are wise. They are thinking of the future state. The nation is fast being de-populated. We must take precautionary measures. We must have men for the future. I warn you, that to do or say anything which subverts the plan of the empire for its own welfare, especially at a time when our national existence is in peril—well, it is treason. Were it not that you are the daughter-in-law of my old friend [*Indicating the Mother*], I should not take the trouble to warn you, but pack you off to jail at once. Not another word from you, you understand?

Hedwig:
[*Calmly, even sweetly, but with fire in her eye.*]

If I say I will keep quiet, will you promise me something in return?

Hertz:

What do you mean? Quiet? Of course you'll keep quiet. Quiet as a tombstone, if I have anything to say about it.

Hedwig:

[*Calm and tense.*]

I mean what I say. Promise to see to it that if we bear you the men for your nation, there shall be no more war. See to it that they shall not go forth to murder and be murdered. That is fair. We will do our part,—we always have,—will you do yours? Promise.

Hertz:

I—I—ridiculous! There will always be war.

Hedwig:

Then one day we will stop giving you men. Look at mother. Four sons torn from her in one month, and none of you ever asked her if she wanted war.   You keep us here helpless. We don't want dreadnoughts and armies and fighting, we women.   You tear our husbands, our sons, from us,—you never ask us to help you find a better way,—and have n't we anything to say?

Hertz:

No.   War is man's business.

Hedwig:

Who gives you the men?   We women.   We bear and rear and agonize.   Well, if we are fit for that, we are fit to have a voice in the fate of the men we bear.   If we can bring forth the men for the nation, we can sit with you in your councils and shape the destiny of the nation, and say whether it is to war or peace we give the sons we bear.

Hertz: [*Chuckling.*]

Sit in the councils? That would be a joke.
I see. Mother, she's a little—[*Touches his
forehead suggestively.*] Sit in the councils
with the men and shape the destiny of the nation! Ha! ha!

Hedwig:

Laugh, Herr Captain, but the day will come;
and then there will be no more war. No, you
will not always keep us here, dumb, silent
drudges. We will find a way.

Hertz:

          [*Turning to the mother.*]

That is what comes of letting Franz go to a
factory town, Maria. That is where he met
this girl. Factory towns breed these ideas.
[*To Hedwig.*] Well, we'll have none of
that here. [*Authoritatively.*] Another word

of this kind of insurrection, another word to
the women of your treason, and you will be
locked up and take your just punishment.
You remember I had to look out for you in the
beginning when you talked against this war.
You 're a firebrand, and you know how we
handle the like of you. [*Goes to ·door, turns
to the mother.*]   I am sorry you have to have
this trouble, Maria, on top of everything else.
You don't deserve it. [*To Hedwig.*]   You
have been warned.   Look out for yourself.

[*Hedwig is standing rigid, with difficulty repress-
ing the torrent of her feelings. Drums are heard
coming nearer, and singing voices of men.*]

Amelia: [*At door.*]

They are passing this way.

Hedwig:

Wave to Arno. Come, Mother. Ah, how
quickly they go!

[*The official steps out of the door. There is quick rhythm of marching feet as the departing regiment passes not very far from the house.*]

There he is! Wave, Mother. Good-by! good-by!

[*The women stand in the doorway, waving their sad farewells, smiling bravely. The sounds grow less and less, until there is the usual silence.*]

In another month, in another week, perhaps, all the men will be gone. We will be a village of women. Not a man left.

[*She leads the old mother into the house once more.*]

Hertz: [*In the door.*]

What did you say?

Hedwig:

Not a man left, I said.

Hertz:

You forget.   *I* shall be here.

Hedwig:

You are old.   You don't count.   They think you are only a woman, Herr Captain.

Hertz: [*Insulted.*]

You—you—

Hedwig:

Oh, don't take it badly, sir. You are honored.   Is the name of woman always to be despised?   Look out in those fields.   Who cleared them, and plucked the vineyards clean? You think we are left at home because we are weak.   Ah, no; we are strong.   That is why. Strong to keep the world going, to keep sacred the greatest things in life—love and home and work. To remind men of—peace. [*With a quick change.*] If only you really were a woman, Herr Captain, that you might breed soldiers for the empire, your glory would be complete.

[*The old captain is about to make an angry reply when there is a commotion outside. The words "News from the front" are distinguished, growing more distinct. The captain rushes out. The women are paralyzed with apprehension for a moment.*]

Mother:

Amelia, go and see. Hedwig, come here.

[*Hedwig crouches on the floor close to the mother, her eyes wide with dread. In a few moments Amelia returns, dragging her feet, woe in her face, and unable to deal the blow which must fall on the two women, who stare at her with blanched faces.*]

Amelia:

[*Falling at her mother's knee.*]

Mother!

Mother:

[*Scarcely breathing.*]

Which one?

Amelia:

All of them.

Mother: [*Dazed.*]

All? All my boys?

Amelia:

Emil, Otto—be thankful Arno is left.

[*The Mother drops her head back against the chair and silently prays. Hedwig creeps nearer Amelia and holds her face between her hands, looking into her eyes.*]

Hedwig:

[*Whispering.*]

Franz?

Amelia:

Franz, too.

[*Hedwig lies prostrate on the floor. Their grief is very silent; terrible because it is so dumb and stoical. The Mother is the first to rouse herself. She bends over Hedwig.*]

Mother:

Hedwig. [*Hedwig sobs . convulsively.*] Don't, child. Be careful for the little one's sake. [*Hedwig sits up.*] For your child be quiet, be brave.

Hedwig:

I loved him so, Mother!

Mother:

Yes, he was my boy—my first-born.

Hedwig:

Your first-born, and this is the end.

[*She rises up in unutterable wrath and despair.*]

O God!

Mother:

[*Anxious for her.*]

Promise me you will be careful, Hedwig. For the sake of your child, *your* first-born, that is to be——

Hedwig:

My child? For this end? For the empire—the war that is to be? No!

Mother:

[*Half to herself.*]

He may look like Franz.

[*Hedwig quickly seizes the pistol from the mantel-shelf and moves to the bedroom door.*

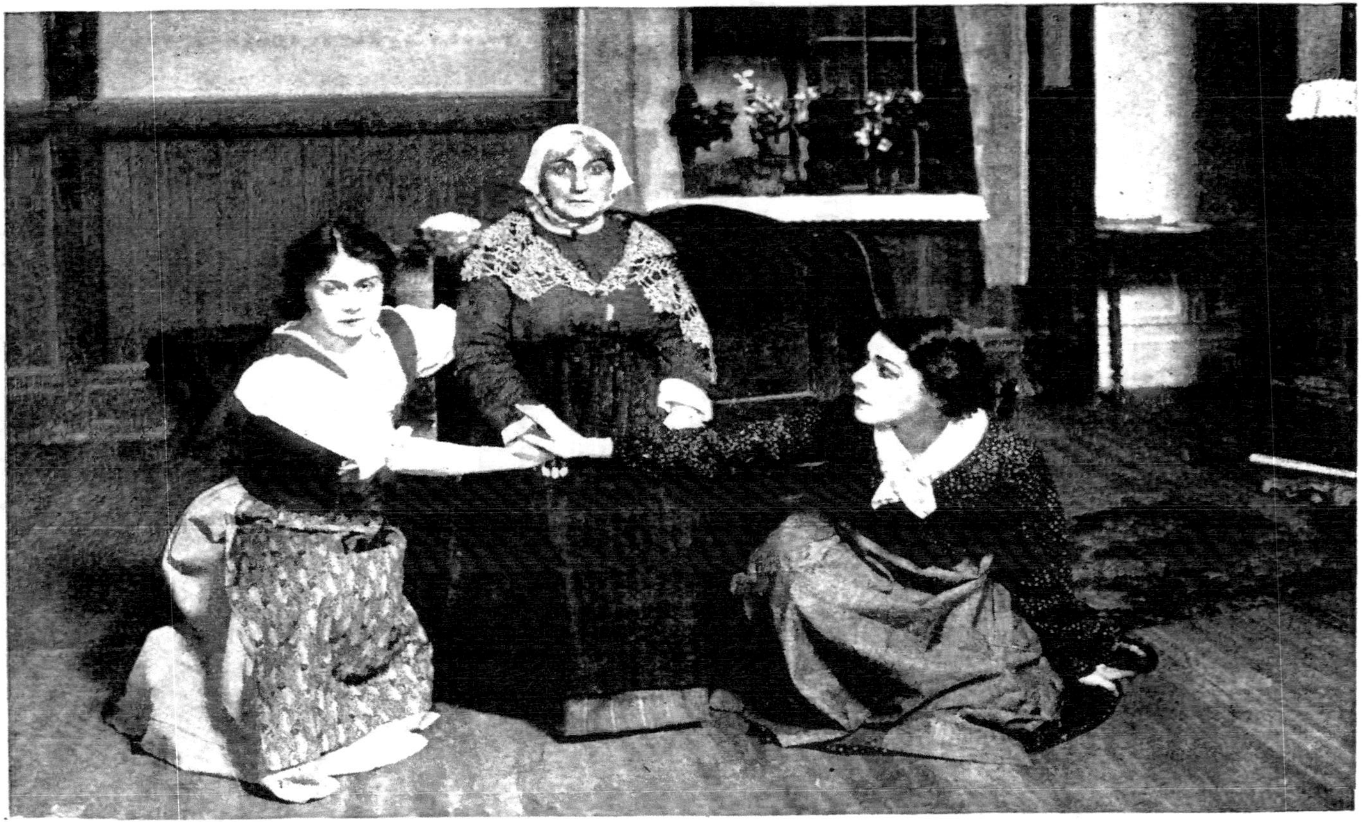

HEDWIG: Franz?

Amelia, watching her, sees her do it, and cries out in alarm and rushes to take it from her.]

Amelia: [*In horror.*]

Hedwig! What are you doing? Give it to me! No, you must not! You have too much to live for.

Hedwig: [*Dazed.*]

To live for? Me?

Amelia:

Why, yes, you are going to be a mother.

Hedwig:

A mother? Like her? [*Looks sadly at the bereaved old mother.*] Look at her! Poor Mother! And they never asked her if she wanted this thing to be! Oh, no! I shall never take it like that—never! But you are right, Amelia. I have something to do first.

[*Lets Amelia put the pistol away in the cupboard.*] I must send a message to the emperor.
[*The others are more alarmed for her in this
mood than in her grief.*]
You said you were going to the front to be a
nurse, Amelia. Can you take this message for
me? I might take it myself, perhaps.

Amelia:

[*Hesitating, not knowing what
to say or do.*]
Let me give you some tea, Hedwig.
[*Voices are heard outside, and the sounds of
sorrow. Some one near the house is weep-
ing. A wild look and a fierce resolve light
Hedwig's face.*]

Hedwig:

[*Rushing from the house.*]
They have taken my Franz!

Mother:

Get her back! I feared it. Grief has made her mad.

[*Amelia runs out. A clamor of voices outside. Hedwig can be heard indistinctly speaking to the women. Finally her voice alone is heard, and in a moment she appears, backing into the doorway, still talking to the women.*]

Hedwig:

[*A tragic light in her face, and hand uplifted.*]

I shall send a message to the emperor. If ten thousand women send one like it, there will be peace and no more war. Then they will hear our tears.

A Voice:

What is the message? Tell us!

Hedwig:

Soon you will know. [*Loudly.*]   But I tell you now, *don't bear any more children* until they promise you there will be no more war.

Hertz:

[*Suddenly appearing.   Amelia follows.*] I heard you. I declare you under arrest. Come with me. You will be shot for treason.

Mother:

[*Fearfully, drawing him aside.*] Don't say that, sir.   Wait.   Oh, no, you can't do that!

[*She gets out her work-basket, and shows him the baby things she has been knitting, and glances significantly at Hedwig. A horrid smile comes into the man's face. Hedwig, snatches the things and crushes them to her breast as if sacrilege had been committed.*]

AMELIA: No, you must not! You have too much to live for.

Hertz:

Is this true? You expect—

Hedwig:

[*Proudly, scornfully.*]
You will not shoot me if I give you a soldier for your empire and your armies and your guns, will you, Herr Captain?

Hertz:

Why—eh, no. Every child counts these times. But we will put you under lock and key. You are a firebrand. I warned you. Come along.

Hedwig:

You want my child, but still you will not promise me what I asked you. Well, we shall see.

Hertz:

Come along.

Hedwig:

Give me just a moment. I want to send a message to the emperor. Will you take it for me, Herr Captain?

Mother: [*Signing.*]

Humor her.

Hertz:

Well, well, hurry up!   .

[*Hedwig sits at table and writes a brief note.*]

Mother: [*Whispering.*]

She has lost Franz. She is crazed.

Hedwig: [*Rising.*]

There. See that it is placed in the hands of the emperor. [*Gives him the note.*] Good-by, Amelia! Never be a war bride, Amelia. [*Kisses her three times,*] Good-by, Mother.

[*Embraces her tenderly.*] Thank you for these.

[*She gathers the baby things in her hands, crosses the room, pressing a little sock to her lips. As she passes the cupboard she deftly seizes the pistol, and moves into the bedroom. On the threshold she looks over her shoulder.*]

Hedwig: [*Firmly.*]
You may read the message out loud.

[*She disappears into the room, still pressing the little sock to her lips.*

Hertz:

[*Reading the note.*]
"A Message to the Emperor: I refuse to bear my child until you promise there shall be no more war."

[*A shot is fired in the bedroom. They rush into the room. The Mother stands trembling by the table.*]

Hertz:

[*Awed, coming out of the room with the baby things, which he places on the table.*]

Dead! Tcha! tcha! she was mad. I will hush it up, Maria.

[*He tears up Hedwig's message to the emperor, and goes out of the house, shaking his head. Amelia is kneeling in the doorway of the bedroom, bending over something, and softly crying. The Mother slowly gathers up the pieces of Hedwig's message and the baby garments, now dashed with blood, and, sitting on the bench, holds them tight against her breast, staring straight in front of her,*

her lips moving inaudibly. She closes her eyes and rocks to and fro, still muttering and praying.]

CURTAIN

Printed by BoD™ in Norderstedt, Germany